This book was made especially for:

✦ COLIN ✦

Dear Colin,

One can't imagine all the places you'll go and amazing things you'll do! Will you build new wonders? Discover new species? Swim in the deepest oceans?

Yes, great adventures lie ahead, and here are 250 words to describe them all. May your life be filled with wonder, magic, and all the good things in this book!

Love,

COLIN *Goes* on a SAFARI

crocodile

tortoise

panther

flamingo

cheetah

gorilla

tiger

monkey

zebra

lion

elephant

giraffe

gazelle

toucan

hippopotamus

warthog

All Around
COLIN'S HOUSE

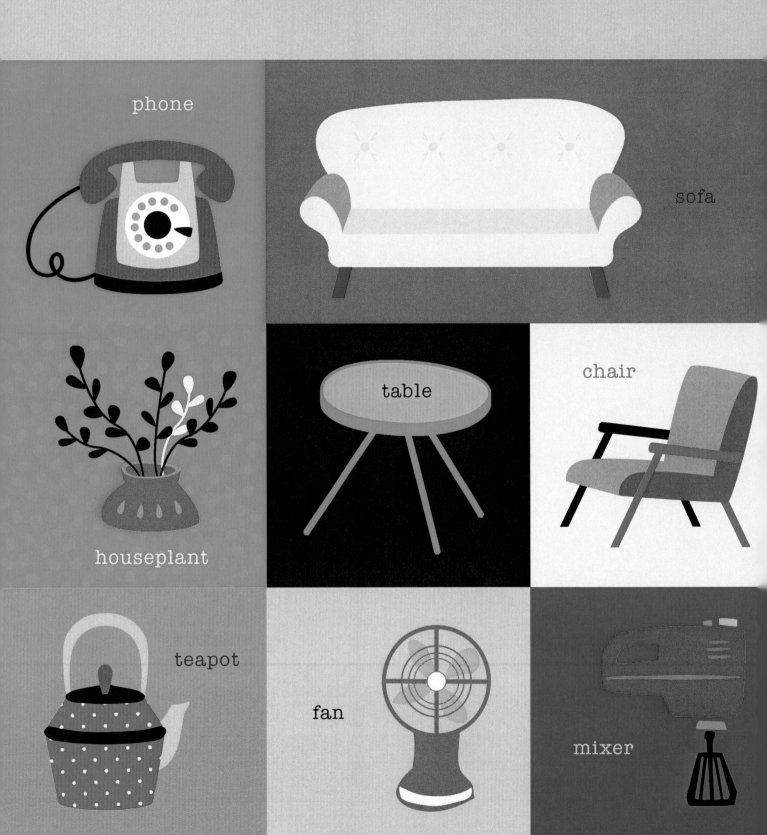

phone

sofa

houseplant

table

chair

teapot

fan

mixer

sewing machine

salt & pepper

clock

television

ladder

lamp

armchair

spatula

rolling pin

blender

Time to EAT, COLIN!

peas

strawberries

lemon

apples

radish

squash

greens

onion

 pear

 tomato

 broccoli

 cucumber

 carrot

 pineapple

 banana

 pepper

COLIN Visits the OCEAN

jellyfish

message
in a
bottle

seagull

lighthouse

fish

crab

sea shells

binoculars

anchor

waves

starfish

coral

seahorse

helm

whale

boat

COLIN *Is* *on the* GO!

bus

car

fire truck

double-decker
bus

garbage truck

roads

monster truck

convertible

truck

dump truck

airplane

tow truck

hot air balloon

taxi

ambulance

helicopter

school bus

ice cream truck

COLIN *Goes* CAMPING

binoculars

canoe

tent

camper

map

mountains

lantern

oars

camp chair

fire

compass

forest

backpack

boots

kayak

flashlight

What's OUTSIDE, COLIN?

sun

puddle

thunderstorm

cloud

rain

snow

umbrella

thermometer

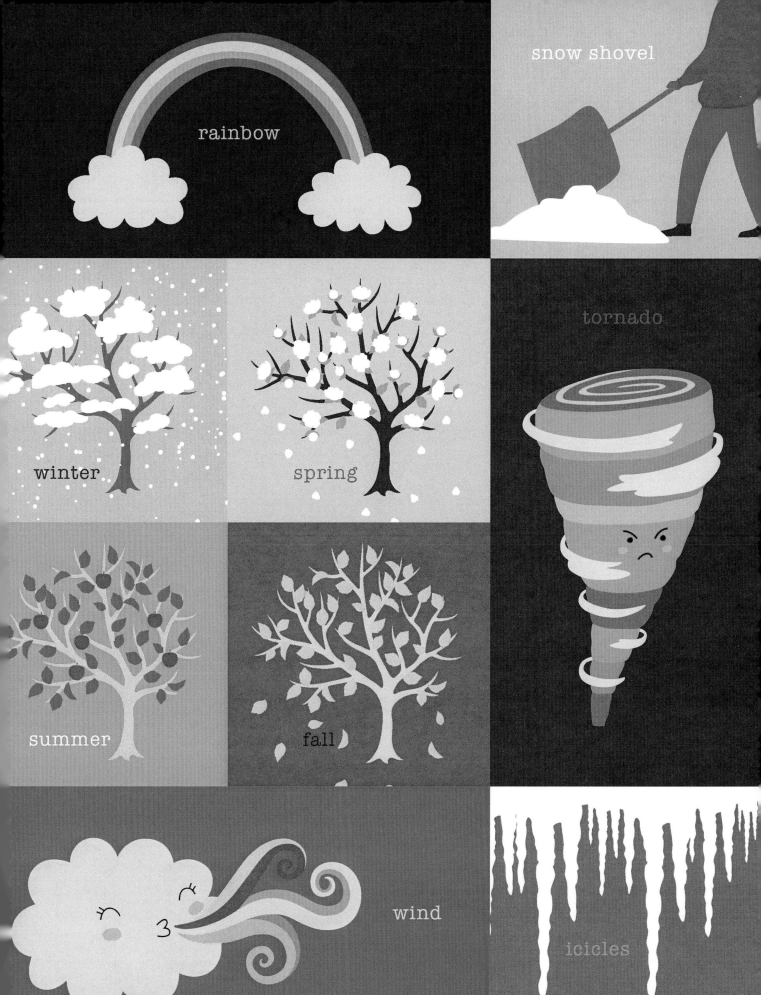

COLIN *in the* GARDEN

basket

gloves

terrarium

pot

boots

hose

watering can

spray bottle

gnomes

shears

seedling

seeds

cut flowers

spade

twine

rake

seedling tray

DINOSAURS
Love COLIN!

cave

Triceratops

Tyrannosaurus

Parasaurolophus

Stegosaurus

amber

jeep

hat

jungle

volcano

Pterodactyl

Diplodocus

Brontosaurus

fossils

dinosaur eggs

footprints

Plesiosaurus

What Will
COLIN BUILD?

caution sign

backhoe

front loader

dirt

house

forklift

bulldozer

steamroller

water truck

 blueprint

 cement mixer

 safety cones

 crane

 skyscraper

 dump truck

 construction workers

 landscaping

COLIN
in the CITY

park

subway

streetlight

city hall

museum

bus

fountain

crosswalk

school

store

taxi

police car

apartment
building

food truck

traffic
light

railroad
tracks

bridge

COLIN Visits the FARM

farmhouse

barn

haystack

windmill

tractor

fields

cow

plate

chickens

dog

crops

chicken coop

sheep

fences

duck

orchard

pig

COLIN'S *in a* FAIRYTALE!

ship

unicorn

magic potion

queen

king

fairy godmother

knight

jester

fox

crystal ball

castle

coach

dragon

 key

cottage

mermaid

mushroom

BATH TIME
for COLIN

soap

towel

rubber duck

toy boat

sponge

plug

faucet

bathtub

conditioner

shampoo

toilet paper

shower

bubbles

soapsuds

comb

SWEET DREAMS,
Dear COLIN

pillow

moon

bedtime stories

dreams

floss

toothbrush

teddy bear

counting
sheep

drink of water

bed

crib

night-light

basinet

bunk bed

constellation

stars

Li'l Llama
CUSTOM KIDS BOOKS

Cover and book design by David Miles

Artwork by the following talented Shutterstock artists: Beskova Ekaterina, Bukhavets Mikhail, Aleksandr Trusov, Sharon Silverman Boyd, KNST ART STUDIO, KateChe, tutti-frutti, Svetlana Kharchuk, GoodStudio, Angelina De Sol, katieromanoff_art, Didou, Nadzin, vectorchef, MirabellePrint, JeedChatt, nemlaza, lena_nikolaeva, Afanasia, ArtMari, IYIKON, metel_m, Alena Razumova, EgudinKa, kulyk, Alexander Ryabintsev, solmariart, Ruslana_Vasiukova, Inkley Studio, Incomible, Ira Bagira, Woodhouse, Andrii Bezvershenko, Follow Art, mckenna71, Ira Che, GoodStudio, tandaV, MG Drachal, Macrovector, Wondermilkycolor, Ksenia Zvezdina, Victor Z, momoforsale, vectortatu, Carboxylase, Kwirry, Buravleva stock, reddish, DoozyDo, Maike Hildebrandt, lyeyee, babystardesign, Kiarnight, Kataryna Lanskaya, Popmarleo, judilyn, Fresh Take Design, NotionPic, NadineVeresk, Sudowoodo, Angelina De Sol, twobears_art, Vector pro, lena_nikolaeva, Olga Zakharova, NadineVeresk, jsabirova, and PinkPueblo.

Made in United States
North Haven, CT
12 July 2022

21250171R00020